11.44

EVANSTON PUBLIC LIBRARY

3 1192 01022 0539

x948.9703 Touba.J

Touba, Jacquiline.

Finland : Anne
   Heinonen's painting

DATE DUE

MAR 1 3 1999	
FEB 0 3 2002	
JAN 1 9 2003	
JUN 0 9 2003	
JUL 2 3 2003	
DEC 0 8 2003	
FEB 0 2 2006 AUG 2 0 2005	
MAR 1 4 2006	

DEMCO, INC. 38-2931

AUG 14 1998

S0-DXO-001

Young Artists of the World™
Finland

Anne Heinonen's Painting: "Life at Home"

Jacquiline Touba, Ph.D. and Barbara Glasser

in collaboration with the IACA World Awareness Children's Museum

The Rosen Publishing Group's
PowerKids Press ™
New York

EVANSTON PUBLIC LIBRARY
CHILDREN'S DEPARTMENT
1703 ORRINGTON AVENUE
EVANSTON, ILLINOIS 60201

The young artist's drawing was submitted to the International Youth Art Exchange program of the IACA World Awareness Children's Museum.
You are invited to contribute your artwork to the museum.
For more details, write to the IACA World Awareness Children's Museum, 227 Glen Street, Glens Falls, NY 12801.
Acknowledgements: Christine Haggblom; Else-Marja Laukkanen.

Published in 1997 by The Rosen Publishing Group, Inc.
29 East 21st Street, New York, NY 10010

Copyright © 1997 by The Rosen Publishing Group, Inc.

All rights reserved. No part of this book may be reproduced in any form without permission in writing from the publisher, except by a reviewer.

First Edition

Book Design: Erin McKenna

Photo Credits: p. 4 © Shinichi Kanno/FPG International Corp.; p. 7 © Walter Bibikow/FPG International Corp.; p. 8 © J. Pickerell/FPG International Corp.; p. 12 © Telegraph Colour Library; pp. 15, 19 © David Bartruff/FPG International Corp.; p. 16 © Marcus Brooke/FPG International Corp.; p. 20 © Hal Kern/International Stock Photography.

Touba, Jacquiline.
    Finland: Anne Heinonen's painting "Life at home"/ by Jacquiline Touba and Barbara Glasser.
        p.   cm. — (Young artists of the world)
    Includes index.
    Summary: The young Finnish artist, Anne Heinonen, describes the culture and traditions of her country, and discusses her painting
of daily life in her city.
    ISBN 0-8239-5101-4
    1. Heinonen, Anne—Juvenile literature. 2. Child artists—Finland—Biography—Juvenile literature. 3. Palkane (Finland) in art—Juvenile literature.
    4. Finns—Ethnic identity—Juvenile literature. [1. Heinonen, Anne. 2. Children's art. 3. Finland—Social life and customs.]
    I. Heinonen, Anne. II. Glasser, Barbara. III. Title. IV. Series.
N352.2.F5T68 1997
948.9703'4—dc21   96-54494
                                                                                CIP
                                                                                AC

Manufactured in the United States of America

Contents

My Family

Terve (TEHR-veh)! That means "hello" in Finnish. My name is Anne Heinonen. I live in **Pälkäne** (PAL-kah-neh), a small village in Finland. I live with my mother in a small block of flats, or apartments, that are two stories high. She works as a salesperson in a store. My father lives in the city of Tampere. Tampere is about 25 miles away from Pälkäne. He works in the metal **industry** (IN-dus-tree).

I don't have any brothers or sisters, but I have a pet. He is a black dwarf rabbit named Jeppe.

Anne Heinonen

◄ This is Helsinki, Finland's largest city. It is much larger than my village of Pälkäne.

5

My City, My Country

My village of Pälkäne is about 100 miles away from Helsinki, the largest city in Finland. Helsinki is also the **capital** (KAP-ih-tul) of my country. Pälkäne is such a beautiful place that many people have summer homes there.

Finland is in the northwest corner of Europe. This area is called Scandanavia. Finland is surrounded by four other countries and the Baltic Sea. Finland is larger than England, Ireland, and Scotland put together! But only slightly more than 5 million people live here. My country is made up of lakes, wetlands, and forests. The Finnish word for Finland is *Suomi* (SOO-oh-me).

In 1808 Helsinki was destroyed by a fire. It was ▶ then rebuilt into the modern city it is today.

The Land

Finland is known as "the land of a thousand lakes." It actually has more than 60,000 lakes, and many of them are connected to each other. We also have thousands of tiny islands along our shores. Almost all of Finland is covered with forests of birch, pine, spruce, and fir trees. The forests are our most important **natural resource** (NA-cher-ul RE-sorss). They are often called "green gold," because many people earn their living from the forest and forest-related industries.

Our forests are beautiful and stay green all year round.

◄ One group of islands, the Aland Islands, is in the Gulf of Bothnia, which separates Finland and Sweden.

I like to play with Tuomo and his cat when I visit with Vera.

My Painting

I painted my picture when I was in the seventh grade. It is called "Life at Home." You can see my friend, Vera, in the painting. She is baby-sitting two little boys, Tuomo and Erkki. They are all watching TV together.

One of my favorite TV shows is called *Moomins*. It is based on the books written by Tove Jansson. But I don't always watch TV. I love to read books after dinner and on the weekends. I like to practice karate, and I love to draw and paint. In the winter I like to go snowboarding. Having good minds and bodies are important to Finns.

Vera baby-sits Tuomo and Erkki a lot. Sometimes ▶
I will visit Vera while she is baby-sitting.

Boys in My Painting

Tuomo is the boy sitting on the couch. He is holding a lollipop and petting his cat, Misu. Tuomo is wearing a **lippalakki** (LEE-pah-lah-kee), which is very popular in Finland. A *lippalakki* is like an American baseball cap. All the young people here wear them.

Tuomo's friend is Erkki. He is wearing the traditional Lapp costume, which is blue, yellow, and red. The Lapps, who call themselves *Saami*, are one of several different groups of people who live in northern Finland. They have their own language, called Lappish. The four peaks in Erkki's hat stand for the northern, southern, eastern, and western winds that blow through Finland.

◀ Some people wear traditional Lapp clothing for holidays. This boy is celebrating Christmas.

Erkki usually only wears his traditional Lapp costume on special occasions.

Vera

Vera's mother helped her make the long black skirt that she wears.

Vera is wearing gold earrings and bracelets. Vera is a Finnish **gypsy** (JIP-see). Gypsies are another group of people that live in Finland. They often move from place to place and stay in small **communities** (kuh-MYOON-ih-teez). They also have their own language.

When gypsy girls turn sixteen years old, they decide if they want to wear the **traditional** (truh-DISH-un-ul) gypsy clothing, or follow other clothing styles in Finland. A gypsy girl's traditional skirt is very heavy. It takes over 30 feet of velvet material to make one skirt. A gypsy may also wear a lace **petticoat** (PET-ee-coht) under her skirt or an apron over it.

This girl is wearing a traditional Finnish costume. ▶

The Land of the Midnight Sun

In northern Finland, there is daylight for 24 hours a day from the middle of May until the end of July. Finland is sometimes called the "land of the midnight sun."

From the night of June 23 through June 24, we celebrate the Midsummer Festival, or the Feast of St. John. We call it **Juhannus** (YUH-hah-nus). At *Juhannus*, we sing, dance, and have huge bonfires outside to keep away evil spirits. The bonfires also help to make sure we have a good harvest and that everyone is healthy in the next year.

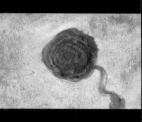

The sunsets in Finland are often orange and red, just like the ball of yarn that the kitten plays with.

◄ Our sunsets can last from two to four hours in one evening!

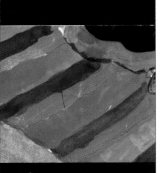

The *rasymatto* in my painting is brightly colored with blue and green cloth.

Crafts

Finland is famous for its wood carvings, fine designs, fabrics, and delicate blown glass. Our love of nature can be seen in our crafts.

In my painting, there is a **rasymatto** (RAH-soo-mah-toh). This is a rug made out of old clothes. The clothes are cut into strips and woven into mats or rugs. Two other traditional weavings are made from wool. They are **ryijy** (REW-ee-yew) and **raanu** (RAH-noo). At one time they were used as bedding or as covers that people wore when they went sleigh riding. Today they are used as wall hangings.

People in Finland often belong to **cooperatives** (koh-OP-ruh-tivz). Finns work together and sell their crafts in these cooperatives.

Crafts, such as these baskets, are sold at nearby flea markets. ▶

The Sauna

Almost every family in Finland has a **sauna** (SAW-nuh). It is built into a house or apartment. Saunas may also be a separate small building next to the house.

A sauna is a small room made entirely of wood. After they shower, the bathers go into the sauna and sit on high wooden benches. Water is thrown over very hot stones, which makes steam. The temperature in a sauna can rise as high as 200°F. To cool off after being in the sauna, bathers will either jump into a cold lake, roll in the snow, or take a cold shower.

◄ To Finns, the sauna is an important part of keeping clean.

Some of the benches in our sauna at home are made of the same wood as the couch in my painting.

My Heritage

Some of the things in our house remind me of my Finnish **heritage** (HEHR-ih-tij) and history. The Finnish flag hangs on one wall. Our flag is white with a blue cross. We also have a copy of the *Kalevela* (KAH-lay-vah-lah). The *Kalevela* is an **epic** (EP-ik) poem that tells the story of Finland and its people. At first it was an **oral** (OR-rul) poem, told over hundreds of years. Then, in 1835, all of its parts were collected by Dr. Elias Lönnrot and made into a book. The *Kalevela* has been translated into more than 30 languages.

I hope you can visit Finland someday. We can celebrate the Midsummer Festival together!

Glossary

capital (KAP-ih-tul) A city in a state or country where the government is located.

community (kuh-MYOON-ih-tee) People living together in one area.

cooperative (koh-OP-ruh-tiv) A group of people working and selling goods together.

epic (EP-ik) A long poem that tells a story.

gypsy (JIP-see) A person who belongs to a group of people who travel from place to place.

heritage (HEHR-ih-tij) The customs and beliefs that are handed down from parent to child.

industry (IN-dus-tree) Any form of business.

Juhannus (YUH-hah-nus) The Finnish word for the Feast of St. John.

Kalevela (KAH-lay-vah-lah) The epic poem about Finland's history.

lippalakki (LEE-pah-lah-kee) A Finnish cap that looks like an American baseball cap.

natural resource (NA-cher-ul RE-sorss) Something in nature that is useful to people.

oral (OR-rul) Spoken.

Pälkäne (PAL-kah-neh) A small village in Finland.

petticoat (PET-ee-coht) A thin skirt worn under another skirt or dress.

raanu (RAH-noo) A Finnish wall hanging made from wool.

rasymatto (RAH-soo-mah-toh) A Finnish rug made from woven strips of cloth.

ryijy (REW-ee-yew) A traditional Finnish hanging made from wool.

sauna (SAW-nuh) A steam bath in which the steam is made by pouring water over hot stones.

Suomi (SOO-oh-me) The Finnish word for Finland.

terve (TEHR-veh) A Finnish word for hello.

traditional (truh-DISH-un-ul) Cultural customs that are handed down from parent to child.

Index